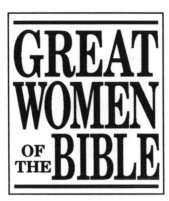

GREAT WOMEN OF THE BIBLE

D1491308

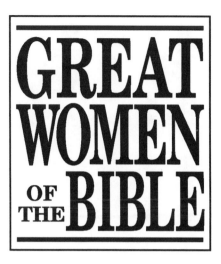

GREAT WOMEN OF THE BIBLE

Clarence E. Macartney

KREGEL PUBLICATIONS
Grand Rapids, Michigan 49501

Great Women of the Bible, by Clarence Edward Macartney, © 1992 by Kregel Publications, P.O. Box 2607, Grand Rapids, Michigan, 49501. This edition includes minor changes in the text and the addition of a new Publisher's Preface and "Questions for Discussion" in each chapter.

Cover Design: Don Ellens
Book Design: Al Hartman

Library of Congress Cataloging-in-Publication Data

Macartney, Clarence Edward Noble, 1879-1957.
  [Great women of the Bible]

Great women of the Bible / Clarence Edward Macartney.
     p.   cm.
  Reprint. Originally published: Great women of the Bible. New York; Nashville : Abingdon-Cokesbury Press, 1942.
  1. Women in the Bible—Sermons. 2. Bible—Biography—Sermons. 3. Sermons. I. Title.
BS575.M29   1992   220.9'22'082—dc20   91-21648
                                                CIP

ISBN 0-8254-3268-5

                2 3 4 5 year / printing 96 95 94 93

Printed in the United States of America

CONTENTS

FOREWORD

I have preached frequently on the great men of the Bible. Some of these sermons appear in the volumes *The Greatest Men of the Bible* and *Sermons on Old Testament Heroes,* and here and there in others. But until recently I have never preached on the great women of the Bible. Quite often I have received requests to do so, but I had some doubts in my mind as to such a course of action. It did not seem at first that the narratives of the women of the Bible had enough of the personal and dramatic element in them to make them the subjects of successful and popular sermons.

But last winter, in answer to many requests, the congregation was given an opportunity to vote on the greatest women of the Bible, just as it had voted on the greatest men. In that vote Ruth stood first in the list, and Eve last. Most of the women dealt with in this volume were on the list of those who received the highest number of votes. However, I have added several women who did not receive a place in the first ten.

As I began to study these characters and to prepare and then preach the sermons, I was agreeably surprised at the way the subject opened up. If anything, the sermons on the great women of the Bible proved more popular than the sermons on the great men of the Bible.

Among the subjects of the sermons in this volume is one of the bad women of the Bible, for no series on women of the Bible would be complete without a sermon on such a character as Delilah, Samson's temptress.

To preach on these biblical women is to illustrate life in its deep reality—sometimes base, ignoble, contemptible, and wicked, but ofttimes lofty, noble, godlike, and glorious. Like the great men of the Bible, too, the great women of the Bible afford the preacher an unsurpassed opportunity to press home upon the people the claims of Christ as Friend and Redeemer.

CLARENCE EDWARD MACARTNEY

PUBLISHER'S PREFACE

D r. Warren W. Wiersbe has said of Clarence Edward Noble Macartney: "His preaching especially attracted men, not only to the Sunday services but also to his popular Tuesday noon luncheons. He was gifted in dealing with Bible biographies, and in this respect, has well been called the 'the American Alexander Whyte.' Much of his preaching was topical-textual, but it was always biblical, doctrinal and practical."

The collection of sermons in this volume admirably fulfill that description. The book, *Great Women of the Bible*, first appeared in 1942. Not only is it an excellent resource for preachers interested in the Bible biographies of "Great Women of the Bible," it will also prove valuable for women's groups and Bible study gatherings interested in learning lessons from the lives of these significant and noteworthy Bible women. Macartney's "sanctified imagination" and deep biblical insight combine to bring these interesting Bible women, famous and infamous, to pulsating life.

The questions for discussion and personal meditation at the end of each chapter are designed to stimulate thought and stir up participation by study groups. Such groups may be large or small and the questions may have to be modified to fit a particular situation. In some cases a regular leader may be required, and in others the leadership role may be passed along from one group member to another. Groups should feel free to adapt or add to the questions as needed because of special circumstances in a given setting.

1

THE WOMAN WHO GOT HER MAN

Thy God shall be my God   (Ruth 1:16).

In the vote of our congregation on the ten greatest women of the Bible, Ruth stood first, and Eve, the first in historical order, stood last. In certain respects I was somewhat surprised at the popularity of Ruth. I had thought that Mary, Sarah, Hannah, Rebekah, or Rachel would take the first place. But the vote was for Ruth.

Why did so many vote for Ruth? Was it because she was an ancestress of our Lord? Was it because of her touching and unusual loyalty to her mother-in-law Naomi? Was it because of the story of how she won Boaz for her husband by that unusual night courtship on the threshing floor? Was it because she firmly and forever chose God and the people of God as her God and her people? Or was it because of the simple beauty and charm of her person and character?

I suppose that all of these factors entered into the choice of the voters. The Book of Ruth is one of the briefest in the Bible, but the portrait it gives us of this Moabitish maiden who came back a young widow to Bethlehem with afflicted and unhappy Naomi is unforgettable.

When Benjamin Franklin went abroad as the representative of

11

the United States in Europe, he would sometimes gather together a fashionable company. Telling them that he had come upon a most remarkable piece of Oriental literature, he would read to them the Book of Ruth. When he had finished, all would express their great delight and ask him how he came upon such a gem of literature. Then he would tell them it was in the Bible. Perhaps some of you have never read the Book of Ruth. If so, I envy you the surprise and joy which are in store for you if you take the trouble, and the few minutes required, to read this great little book.

The story of Ruth is an idyl of domestic love which comes between the books of Judges and Samuel, so filled with war and murder and cruelty. It is a sweet interlude of peace and love in a fierce, wild chorus of war and passion. In this book not a single wicked, cruel, or licentious person makes his appearance. Here we behold the attractiveness of virtue, the beauty of sacrifice, and the winsomeness of simple trust in God.

A TALE OF THREE WIDOWS

The story of Ruth is a tale of three widows. Out of Bethlehem, where Christ was to be born, driven by the famine, Elimelech, his wife Naomi, and their two sons, Mahlon and Chilion, had migrated, not westward, as families and races have done through the ages, but eastward, across the Jordan to the land of Moab, where God was not known. But in that land they were doomed to disappointment.

Life was even harder there than it had been in Bethlehem. First Elimelech, the head of the family, sickened and died. And then, ten years after, the two sons died, leaving Naomi alone with her two heathen daughters-in-law, Orpah and Ruth.

Sorrow as well as joy turns the heart homeward and to the scenes of youth. It was not strange, then, that in her sorrow Naomi turned homeward to Bethlehem. Her two daughters-in-law determined to go with her; but when they came to the river Jordan, the dividing line between the two countries, Naomi, beautiful and unselfish, begged the two young widows to go back to Moab. They could not know as she did, she told them, how hard life was in a strange land. Moreover, it would be difficult for them to find husbands in Bethlehem. If they went with her, they would share those sorrows which God had brought upon them.

Hearing that, Orpah kissed her mother-in-law and turned back to Moab. But Ruth refused to leave her. She answered Naomi in these immortal words—and what she said ranks among the most beautiful sayings of all the Bible—"Entreat me not to leave thee, or to return from following after thee: for whither thou goest, I will go; and where thou lodgest, I will lodge: thy people shall be my people, and thy God my God: where thou diest, will I die, and there will I be buried: the Lord do so to me, and more also, if aught but death part thee and me" (Ruth 1:16,17). Sometimes, where it seems appropriate, I use that matchless affirmation of Ruth in the marriage service. Indeed, that last phrase, "If aught but death part thee and me," is the origin of the familiar marriage affirmation, "Till death us do part."

A PRETTY GLEANER IN THE FIELDS

There had been great changes in Bethlehem during the years of Naomi's absence in Moab. When the familiar landmarks came into view I imagine her heart beat high with hope. There again was her native land and her native village. But there were sad memories too. She recalled the day she had set out with her family for Moab with great expectations of the future. People did not migrate much in those days, and the departure or the return to or from a far country was an event in the monotonous life of the village.

The whole town turned out when they heard that Naomi was coming home. They remembered her as the young and beautiful wife of Elimelech, the fairest woman in the village. But when they saw this travel-stained woman with the marks of sorrow and advancing years upon her, they could hardly believe it was Naomi. "Is this Naomi?" the villagers asked one another as they gathered around her and looked upon her faded beauty. Naomi means "Pleasantness." But Naomi, recognizing the change in her person and her lot, answered the wondering women: "Call me not Naomi, call me Mara [Bitterness]: for the Almighty hath dealt very bitterly with me. I went out full, and the Lord hath brought me home again empty: why then call ye me Naomi?" (Ruth 1:20-21).

Although she had met with adversity and misfortune, Naomi was not soured or embittered by her lot, for she reverently recognized the hand of God in her life.

They were harvesting the barley at Bethlehem when Naomi and Ruth returned. The harvest was, and still is, the one great social and economic event in that land where men must have bread.

If the villagers had wondered at the faded charms of Naomi, they had not failed to mark the fair and womanly grace of the Moabite girl who accompanied her. Although of a foreign, idol-worshiping race, Ruth soon made friends among her new people whose lot and God she had chosen. There were no men in the household to go into the fields and toil, and they had no fields of their own where others could toil for them. But Ruth, realizing the situation, and Naomi's and her own need, asked permission of her mother-in-law to go into the fields and glean after the reapers.

The Old Testament was by no means all law and severity. Strands of mercy and compassion ran through the fabric of the Hebrew jurisprudence, and one of these strands was the law of the harvest that the poor and the needy could glean after the reapers. In that way they could gather what was necessary for their sustenance. The corners of the fields were not to be wholly gleaned, nor the fruit trees picked or beaten twice. Always something was to be left for the foreigner and the poor. Being both poor and a foreigner, Ruth was certain of consideration at the hands of the reapers.

Ruth could not have known that morning all it was to mean to her; but when she went forth to glean it was her good fortune to glean that part of the field belonging to Boaz, who was connected by blood with the family of Naomi's husband. She had hoped and prayed for favor in the eyes of some kindhearted man. Her prayer was answered.

There is Ruth, then, following the reapers up and down the fields of Boaz. If you have seen the reapers and the threshers at work in Palestine, it will not be difficult for you to picture the scene, or even if you have paintings or photographs of it. What strikes one today is the variety of the colors worn by the women. As I remember it now, yellow, red, and blue were the prevailing colors, the headdress of the women being the most conspicuous part of their attire. I fancy that Ruth did not forget to array herself in the most becoming colors that morning when she went forth to glean. Naomi probably took a hand, too, and tried this or that scarf about Ruth's head and brow before they finally decided upon the one which best suited her style of beauty. From what follows it is plain that they made no mistake.

In his beautiful "Ode to a Nightingale," John Keats imagines Ruth listening to the entrancing song of that bird in the fields at Bethlehem:

> Perhaps the self-same song that found a path
> Through the sad heart of Ruth, when, sick for home,
> She stood in tears amid the alien corn.

But I think Keats missed it when he spoke of Ruth as "sick for home." Ruth had willingly and gladly chosen Israel and turned her back on Moab and its idols forever.

As the day advances, here came the mowers swinging their sickles, and the reapers gathering up the grain and binding it into bundles. Men had done this from the dawn of history, until one day a young farmer in Rockbridge County, Virginia, had an idea, and the reaper was invented. Today on the campus of Washington and Lee University at Lexington there stands a monument to that young man, Cyrus McCormick. On the monument are cut these words, "He lifted the burden from the back of labor."

At length Boaz appears on the scene to see how the work progresses. The greetings which passed between employer and employees showed the character of Boaz and the happy relationship which existed. "The Lord be with you," Boaz said to the reapers, who answered, "The Lord bless thee."

A WOMAN PROPOSES

Boaz may have been a bachelor, and perhaps well along in years, but he did not fail to note the presence of the strange young woman. He looked upon her with admiring eye as he watched her bend her lithesome young body with infinite grace as she gleaned after the reapers. Calling the foreman to him, Boaz said to him, "Who is that damsel?" When he was told that it was the Moabite girl who had come back with Naomi, he called her to him and told her not to glean elsewhere, but to stay in his fields, where she would receive every consideration.

When Ruth expressed surprise that she had found such grace in his eyes, Boaz said to her that he had heard of her kindness and loyalty to her mother-in-law and prayed that God would bless her. In beautiful language he said, "A full reward be given thee of the Lord God of Israel, under whose wings thou art come to trust" (Ruth 2:12).

When Ruth went back to join the reapers, Boaz charged them to deal kindly with her, and in addition to what was generally left, to drop some "handfuls on purpose" for her to glean. The result was that when Ruth went back that night to Naomi she took with her an ephah of barley. And much more than an ephah of barley, too: Ruth carried home the heart of Boaz; for wisely, unlike Whittier's judge, who saw Maud Muller in the meadow and sighed, and rode by, Boaz appeared at the field every day Ruth came to glean.

Naomi asked her where she had gleaned; and when Ruth told her it was in the field of Boaz, Naomi, knowing that Boaz was a kinsman to her husband, cried out in joy, "Blessed be he of the Lord, who hath not left off his kindness to the living and to the dead" (Ruth 2:20). Every day Ruth went to glean in the fields of Boaz, and every day Boaz saw her and his heart warmed toward her.

At length, one day as the harvest season was drawing to a close, the wise Naomi, seeing that Boaz was fond of Ruth, and that Ruth herself was not unwilling, made to Ruth the suggestion that she go to Boaz and ask him to marry her.

We must view that plan and plot of Naomi's in the light of their ancient custom: if a man died leaving his wife, and without a child, it was the duty of the nearest kinsman to marry her. Ruth's dead husband, Mahlon or Chilion, whichever it was, was a kinsman of Boaz, and this fact lay back of Naomi's plot. It would certainly be awkward, and often unpleasant, if law and custom required men to marry the widows of their relatives, for all are not like Ruth. But in those days the continuity of the family and the nation, rather than the individual, was the important thing.

Following the directions of Naomi, Ruth arrayed herself in her most attractive garments; and that night after Boaz had lain down to sleep on one of his threshing floors, a custom still followed in order to guard the grain against theft, she came softly down the threshing floor. In a part of the floor removed from the others Boaz lay sleeping. Silently, in her bare feet, Ruth made her way over the soft piles of the grain, stopping now and then and sinking down with fear when one of the sleeping reapers stirred uneasily in his slumber. At length she came to where Boaz slept, and lay down at his feet.

At midnight Boaz awoke and, turning himself, was amazed and frightened to see a woman lying at his feet. "Who art thou?" he exclaimed. Ruth replied: "I am Ruth thine handmaid: spread therefore thy skirt over thine handmaid; for thou art a near kinsman" (Ruth 3:9). When Boaz heard that, his heart leaped with joy that Ruth had been unmindful of the many young men nearer her own age and had set her affections upon him.

Boaz was immediately willing. But his first thought was for Ruth's reputation and for his own good name; and that should be uppermost in the mind of every man and every woman. He told Ruth that if a kinsman nearer to her than he was would not marry her, he would gladly do so. That they could ascertain when the day came. It would not do for the reapers to know that a woman had come by night to the threshing floor. That might ruin the reputation of both of them. He, therefore, told her to lie quiet till the day was beginning to break. Then, when it was still dark enough so that no one could be recognized, Ruth arose, and taking with her six measures of grain that the generous Boaz had poured into her veil, she left the threshing floor and returned to her mother-in-law.

Naomi's plan was a bold one, and had certain dangers; but it worked well and Ruth got her man, and never did a woman get a better one; for Boaz was a man of high sense of honor, virtuous, godly, generous, and kind. Young women who are following in the steps of Ruth and seeking a husband would do well to consider if the man in question has some of the traits of Boaz.

A faint heart never won a fair husband. All's well that ends well. Probably Boaz, the old bachelor, would never have had the courage himself to seek the hand of Ruth. That night God worked in a mysterious way His wonders to perform. But two hearts were made happy. A true godly home was established, and a child was born and a son was given. They called his name Obed. He became the father of Jesse, and Jesse was the father of David, and of the line of David came Christ.

PROVIDENCE AND HUMAN LIFE

This famous story yields two great and timeless truths. The first of these is the fact of God's providence in our lives. Every one of the characters of the Book of Ruth reverently owns the presence of God in life and human affairs: Naomi who saw the hand of God in her sorrow and adversity; Boaz who recognized the hand of God in the good fortune that gave him Ruth for a wife; and Ruth herself who, as Boaz expressed it, put her trust under the wings of the Lord God of Israel.

The record reads that when Ruth went out that morning to glean, "her hap was to light on a part of the field belonging unto Boaz." The whole story with its great sequence turns upon that "hap," that chance. Had it been some other field, the history would have been different. But it was the field of Boaz, the kinsman of her dead husband's family. Through that circumstance Ruth became the ancestress of Jesus Christ, the Savior of her soul and the Redeemer of mankind,

Great events turn upon the hinges of little happenings. Ruth could not have told why, when she went forth that morning to glean and looked over the fields where the reapers were at work, she turned to the left or right and chose the field belonging to Boaz. With her it was only a coincidence, but God was with her. God guided her footsteps that morning.

When you look back you see how life has been made up of happenings like that. Had you gone east instead of west, taken a morning train instead of an evening train, gone around another corner, met another person, life could not have been what it has been. Faith will recognize God's hand not only in the obviously pleasant things of life, such as the bringing together of Ruth and Boaz, but also in what are termed the hard things of life.

As life wore on for Robert Louis Stevenson, his faith became stronger in what he called "the kindness of the scheme of things and the goodness of our veiled God." To his father he wrote:

There is a fine text in the Bible, I don't know where,[1] to the effect that all things work together for good to those who love the Lord. . . . Strange as it may seem to you, everything has been, in one way or another, bringing me a little nearer to what I think you would like me to be. . . . Tis a strange world, indeed, but there is a manifest God for those who care to look for Him.

And a greater than Stevenson said:

> There's a divinity that shapes our ends,
> Rough-hew them how we will.[2]

DECISION AND DESTINY

The other great truth which the Book of Ruth illustrates so dramatically is the power of choice and decision. Ruth chose definitely and forever the people of God. Her decision was given in that immortal declaration, "Entreat me not to leave thee: . . . thy people shall be my people, and thy God my God." When Naomi announced her intention to go back to Bethlehem, both of her daughters-in-law said they would go with her, and both started back with her. But when they reached the boundary line between the two countries, the river Jordan, Orpah yielded to the entreaties of Naomi and, kissing her mother-in-law, went back to Moab.

She represents a common type that abound in all our churches: people who have some real desire to go with Christ and His people, but who never bring themselves to the point of breaking with the world. Their hearts are in Moab, and eventually back to Moab they go.

But Ruth stands for those whose decision is final and irrevocable. There is no turning back, no backward look even, toward Moab, toward the life of the world. There she stands on the bank of the river Jordan, with her back to Moab, and on her lips that grand decision and choice, "Whither thou goest, I will go; . . . thy people shall be my people, and thy God my God."

Decision, choice, that is the first step in the Christian life. Have you taken that step? Have you made that decision? Have you

---

1. Romans 8:28.
2. William Shakespeare, *Hamlet*, V, 2.

chosen Jesus Christ and Eternal Life? Great things hung that day on Ruth's choice, and not less great—even the destiny of an immortal soul—hang upon your decision. Will you say the word now? While all the angels listen and all the redeemed give thanks—say it to Him who loved you and died for you, "Entreat me not to leave thee, or to return from following after thee."

QUESTIONS FOR DISCUSSION:

1. Why do you think Ruth was the most popular Bible character in Dr. Macartney's poll? Would the same factors hold true today?

2. Does it ever help to run away from a problem as Elimelech and his family did in moving to Moab?

3. Why is Ruth's pledge of loyalty, "entreat me not to leave thee . . ." (Ruth 1:16,17), so popular as a wedding vow? Read these verses in several modern versions and discuss.

4. What was the difference between Ruth's commitment to Naomi and Orpah's?

5. Why do you suppose Dr. Macartney assumes that Boaz was an older man?

6. Discuss the reason (or reasons) why Ruth proposed to Boaz—or did she?

7. Do you agree with Dr. Macartney's evaluation of the characters of Ruth and Orpah at the end of the chapter?

Editor's Note: In preparation for this study, read the book of Esther carefully, noting particularly the clues to the various characters who take leading roles in this drama.

2

THE WOMAN WHOSE BEAUTY SAVED A RACE

And if I perish, I perish   (Esther 4:16).

"Beauty," the wise man said, "is vain." But it is not always so. Not when beauty of face and body is joined to beauty of soul. There is a beauty which can inflame and destroy men. History tells of one woman whose beauty dyed the seas with blood and almost destroyed two nations. That was the disastrous influence of the beauty of Helen of Troy—

> . . . . the face that launch'd a thousand ships,
> And burnt the topless towers of Ilium.[1]

But here we have the story of how God used the beauty of one woman to save a nation from destruction and carry forward His eternal purpose.

The story of Esther is a drama that opens with a banquet which for wickedness and beauty and splendor and length of time has rarely, if ever, been surpassed. It is midnight in the palace of Ahasuerus, the king of Persia and the despot of the world. By

---

1. Christopher Marlowe, *Doctor Faustus*, scene xiv.

some he has been identified with that Xerxes who crossed the Hellespont with a great army, forced the pass at Thermopylae and then marched on south through Greece, only to see his invasion checked and his fleet destroyed at the battle of Salamis Bay. I have visited the rocky eminence near Salamis where Xerxes sat and watched his fleet perish in the waters of the Aegean.

> A king sate on the rocky brow
> Which looks o'er sea-born Salamis;
> And ships, by thousands, lay below,
> And men and nations;—all were his!
> He counted them at break of day—
> And when the sun set where were they?[2]

SETTING THE SCENE

Ahasuerus sits in royal state at the center of the table in the great banqueting hall, and all about him are ranged the 127 princes of his far-flung empire. This convocation of the satraps of Ahasuerus probably took place at the very time when he was planning his ill-starred invasion of Greece. For 180 days, or six months, the king has been engaged in showing these assembled satraps the riches of his glorious kingdom and the honor of his excellent majesty. For the last seven days a great banquet has been in operation. Ahasuerus is flanked by his 127 princes, all gorgeously arrayed in their resplendent robes, with their gems and jewels and tiaras flashing in the light that glows from the myriad candles and the vast candelabra that hang from the ceiling. The floor of the banquet hall is black, white, blue, and red marble. Marble columns hold up the roof, from which is suspended a vast canopy of blue, green, and white velvet, fastened with cords of fine linen to silver rings inserted in the marble columns. The beds, or couches, on which the revelers recline are in keeping with the splendor of all else that night, for they are of silver or gold, decorated with the beasts and deities of Persian superstition and wickedness. Every cup out of which the banqueters are drinking is of purest gold, and each cup is wrought and chased with a different design.

---

2. Byron, *Don Juan*, iii, 87.

Slaves and eunuchs, black as the marble tiles of the palace floor, pass to and fro with the food and the liquors. In the minstrels' galleries sensuous music floats down, with the strains of the harp, psaltery, timbrel, flute, cornet, sackbut, and dulcimer mingling their strains. Fountains throw their spray up from their basins, and the sweet incense of Persia, India, and Ormuz fills the air.

On a central platform dancing girls, their flimsy garments disclosing the wanton beauty of their bodies, whirl beguilingly about in the Oriental dance. Seven days have passed, and they are still eating and drinking and dancing. Many have been overcome by drink and fatigue and are being carried out by their slaves on litters.

Ahasuerus is thinking to himself, *What more can I do to entertain and excite these guests?* Then to his alcohol-inflamed brain comes a new idea. "The queen! The beauty of all the earth! I will bring in Vashti and display her beauty to my satraps and their ladies." Summoning his seven chamberlains, Mehuman, Carcas, Zethar, and the others, he commands them in his drunken voice to bring in Vashti.

VASHTI REFUSES THE KING'S SUMMONS

Significantly, the sacred chronicler records that it was when the heart of Ahasuerus was inflamed with wine that he made his shameful and infamous proposal concerning Vashti the queen. That is the old, old history of strong drink, ever since it left Noah, God-fearing Noah, uncovered and debauched in the presence of his sons, and by the very altar which he had built to God.

However commonplace and fashionable it may be to drink liquor, let it be remembered that the effect of liquor is to stir up the lower passions of one's nature and to relax the soul's watch over its safety. In a moment of such relaxation, when the stimulation of strong drink has weakened the natural resistance to evil, young men and young women have written a record of sorrow or of shame which can never be reversed.

Startled by so wicked and unprecedented a proposal, the drunken lords sat up in eagerness to await the coming of the far-famed queen. But they were doomed to disappointment, and Ahasuerus to futile rage; for Vashti refused to come in. She refused to expose herself to the lascivious gaze of Ahasuerus and his drink-inflamed satraps. Vashti said "No"—one of the great God-inspired "Nos" of all history.

Let all women remember that "No." Vashti had world-famed beauty; but she lives forever in history, not because she had beauty, but because she had character, had respect for herself, without which the fairest beauty is but as a jewel in a swine's snout. She counted the cost—dismissal from the court, exile, perhaps death itself—but she loved honor, loved her soul, more than life itself. That "No" made Vashti immortal, and it made Esther immortal too; for, as we shall see, had it not been for the "No" of Vashti, Esther would never have been heard of.

ENTER ESTHER

Esther has societies and guilds and women named after her. But if I had a daughter I think I should like to name her Vashti.

Vashti's refusal lost her the crown. Now a new queen, a new favorite had to be chosen. Annually today there is still held at Atlantic City the Miss America pageant. Here was the original beauty contest, not of a city, or state, or nation, but of the whole world. Every province of Ahasuerus' empire was combed for its most beautiful women, those who might be presented at the court as possible candidates for the crown of the queen of Persia. The choice fell on a young woman named Esther. Her Hebrew name was Hadassah, which means "myrtle"; but her Persian name was Esther, which means "a star." And a star Esther was, not only in physical beauty, but in beauty of soul.

This girl was a Jewess, the adopted daughter of her cousin, Mordecai, who had a post of some importance at the palace. He himself played a part in putting forward his lovely cousin to be the queen of Ahasuerus. So it came about that the beautiful Hebrew girl became the favorite and queen of the king of the whole earth.

Among the ministers of Ahasuerus—and now the villain of this drama—was a man named Haman. By merit he had risen to his post of prime minister. Whenever he entered or left the king's palace everyone did him reverence and bowed down—all but one man, Mordecai, who bowed not nor did him reverence. "Yet all this availeth me nothing, so long as I see Mordecai the Jew sitting at the king's gate," said Haman (Esther 5:13).

Mordecai spells character. He had principles; and, like Daniel, he was true to them. His conscience forbade him to bow down and do reverence to a wicked man like Haman, and he obeyed his conscience. Without character, without loyalty to principle, man is but a beast or a clod.

Haman never forgot the insult of Mordecai, and to avenge himself he ruined his happiness, his fortune, and lost life itself. To his wife he said, after he had been honored by an invitation to the banquet with Ahasuerus and the queen, "Yet all this availeth me nothing, so long as I see Mordecai the Jew sitting at the king's gate."

Here was a man who had next to the highest post in the world. From the Persian Gulf to the Caspian Sea, and from the Mediterranean to India there was not a jewel, a horse, a camel, a garment, a fruit, a woman, that Haman could not have for the asking; but all that went for nothing as long as he saw Mordecai, the Jew, refusing to do him honor. That spoiled everything for him.

He forgot everything he had and centered his mind on the one thing he could not have—the reverence of Mordecai. One fly in his dish caused the whole ointment of his life to stink. But if Haman was a fool for permitting one non-bowing and dissenting Jew to ruin his happiness, he was a greater fool to permit his anger and humiliation to move him to revenge and murder.

HAMAN THE HATER

To satisfy his hurt pride and feed his hatred Haman planned a ferocious vengeance which was to embrace the whole race of Jews to which Mordecai belonged, and in addition a particular vengeance upon Mordecai himself. Now watch the sequence of sin in Haman's heart—first pride, then revenge, then falsehood, and finally murder.

He told Ahasuerus that the nonconforming Jews scattered throughout all his kingdom were the cause of all the troubles that arose in his empire. That has a very modern sound to it. Perhaps that is where Hitler got the idea. Since it is recorded that both of them sat down to drink afterward, I think there can be little doubt that Ahasuerus was drunk when Haman got him to stamp with his signet ring the infamous edict that on the thirteenth day of the twelfth month all Jews in every province of the empire were to be put to the sword.

Then Haman, at the suggestion of his wife, planned a particular revenge upon Mordecai. A gallows fifty cubits high was erected, and at the set time Haman was going to hang Mordecai on that gallows. All was ready. There could be no slip. The edict for the massacre of the Jews was signed, and there was the gallows, fifty cubits high, its rope swinging in the night wind, waiting for the neck of Mordecai.

But there was Another, whom neither king nor Haman had taken into the reckoning. Behind them the dim unknown God was standing, keeping watch above His own. The gallows Haman had erected for Mordecai is going to sway the future.

The night before Mordecai was to die Ahasuerus could not sleep. Perhaps another seven-day banquet was the reason for his sleeplessness. To pass the tedium of the sleepless night, Ahasuerus summoned his secretaries to read to him from the chronicles of his reign. As they read they came to a passage which related how Mordecai had saved Ahasuerus from assassination at the hands of two of his chamberlains. When the king learned that no reward had been given Mordecai for thus saving his life, he resolved to give him some signal recognition. He was debating how he should do this when there came a knock at his door. It was Haman—wicked, cruel, confident Haman—come to ask permission to hang Mordecai.

When Haman had come in, Ahasuerus, evidently suspicious now as to Haman's motives, craftily asked him, "What shall be done unto the man whom the king delighteth to honor?" *And whom*, thought Haman, *could the king delight to honor more than myself?* Therefore, he suggested to the king that such a man be arrayed in royal robes, mounted on the king's Arabian charger, and conducted thus through the streets of the capital, with the man who led the horse crying out to the multitude, "Thus shall it be done to the man whom the king delighteth to honor." Then the king said, "Thou art the man! Take my horse and mount Mordecai on it, and lead him in procession through the streets."

Crestfallen and terrified, Haman did as the king commanded and led his enemy in triumph through the city. As he passed down one street he saw the gallows, fifty cubits high, which he had erected for Mordecai, the rope swinging in the morning breeze. When he saw that fear gripped Haman's wicked heart, and he thought to himself, watching that gallows, *Mordecai the Jew got the ride on the king's horse instead of me. What if I were to get the ride on the gallows instead of Mordecai!*

That was one movement of Divine Providence—God acting through the sleepless king and the chance reading of a page from the royal chronicles. The other agency through which God acted to save Israel from annihilation was the beauty and spirit of Esther.

As soon as Mordecai learned of the edict that had gone forth for the slaughter of his race, he covered himself with sackcloth and ashes and sat in mourning at the gates of the palace. Word of this was brought to the queen, who sent a messenger to Mordecai inquiring of him the reason for this act of public mourning. Then Mordecai disclosed to her the wicked plot of Haman and besought her to go to the king, Ahasuerus, and plead for the life of her people. That Esther was a Jewess had thus far been kept secret at the court.

Not unnaturally, Esther feared to go into the presence of the king unsummoned. That was what assassins tried to do, and whoever came unbidden into the presence of the king was immediately put to death. Esther reminded her cousin and foster father of the law and custom. Mordecai's answer is one of the great sayings of the Bible and of history: "For if thou altogether holdest thy peace at this time, then shall there enlargement and deliverance arise to the Jews from another place; but thou and thy father's house shall be destroyed: and who knoweth whether thou art come to the kingdom for such a time as this?" (Esther 4:14).

ESTHER'S VOW

That noble sentence struck a chord deep in Esther's breast. If it was God's will that she go in to the king, she would go. If it was God's plan to save her race through her plea before Ahasuerus, she was ready to make that plea. Asking for a fast—that is, the prayers of all Jews—Esther answered Mordecai's noble sentence with one of her own, equally noble: "So will I go in unto the king, which is not according to the law: and if I perish, I perish" (Esther 4:16).

The issue of her daring and faith was that the king extended to her the royal scepter when she came in, the sign of the royal favor, and promised to do whatever she desired.

For answer, Esther said, "Let the king and Haman come this day unto the banquet that I have prepared for him" (Esther 5:4). At the banquet that night and in the presence of Haman, the king said again to Esther, "What is thy petition? . . . and what is thy request? even to the half of the kingdom it shall be performed" (Esther 5:6). But again Esther hesitates. She does not yet tell the king what her heart desires—the salvation of her people—but only requests that the king and Haman come to another banquet, which she will serve on the morrow.

Why did Esther delay to state her request? Perhaps she was hoping that there would be some happening, some event, which would strengthen her request and ensure its success. An inward voice may have told her, "Do not state your request tonight, but wait until tomorrow night." But whether Esther understood the significance of her request or not, certain it is that the hand of God was in that delay; for it was on that night—the night before the second banquet—that the king could not sleep, and learned of the service that Mordecai had rendered him in saving him from assassination. Then, in the caprice of his royal mind, he ordered Haman to show great honor to Mordecai. Thus the mind of the king was providentially prepared to grant the request of his beautiful queen.

On the night of the second banquet, the king again asked for her request. This time Esther did not hesitate, but said, "O king, and if it please the king, let my life be given me at my petition, and my people at my request: for we are sold, I and my people, to be destroyed, to be slain, and to perish" (Esther 7:3). The amazed king, apparently forgetful of the edict he had signed, probably when he was drunk, exclaimed, "Who is he, and where is he, that durst presume in his heart to do so?" Then Esther, rising in all her majesty, and pointing to the cowering Haman said, "The adversary and enemy is this wicked Haman" (Esther 7:6). When the king heard that, he gave the order that Haman should be hanged on the gallows fifty cubits high, that he had built for Mordecai. Thus, the beauty and courage of Esther saved her race from annihilation.

PROVIDENCE IN THE LIVES OF MEN AND NATIONS

The first great truth that is brought home to us by the Book of Esther and the history of Esther is that God's purpose is being carried out in this world in the lives of men and nations, and that the plan by which God works is His divine providence. Some have been troubled about this book of the Bible because the name of God nowhere appears in its pages. Some have tried to explain this absence of the name of God from a book in God's Word on the ground that the Hebrew author of the book, living in the midst of the heathen people, found it wise to omit from his history the secret of Israel's deliverance, knowing the while that all Jews would not miss the meaning of the book. Others have claimed to find that name of God in an acrostic form in the Hebrew words.

But the absence of the name of God need not trouble us. If the name of God is not there, the Fact, the Power, the Presence of God, is there. No book of the Bible teaches the sovereignty and the providence of God more clearly. In reality, the name of God is written large on every page of the book.

And in how strange a way, and through what apparently trifling incidents the purpose of God works in the world! Here God uses the insomnia of a king and the chance reading of a page from the royal chronicles to set in motion events which saved Mordecai from death and saved Israel from death.

Here we see how God works through the free and voluntary acts of men, good and bad, to carry forward His purposes. So far as Ahasuerus was concerned, it was just a chance, a happenstance that he was unable to sleep the night before the day set for the hanging of Mordecai; and it was only a chance event again that when his secretaries read to him that night, they opened to the very page where was written the story of how Mordecai had saved him from assassination.

But what is a chance event? Is there any chance event with God? Pharaoh's daughter went down to bathe one morning in the Nile River and chanced upon that part of the river where Moses lay sleeping in his cradle in the bulrushes, and Moses was saved to deliver Israel out of the house of Egypt and the land of bondage. Columbus, nearing the American continent, turned southwest to follow the flight of birds and thus came to South America; hence North America was reserved for Anglo-Saxon and Protestant settlement.

John Bunyan was drafted to stand as a sentinel when Cromwell's army was besieging an English city—probably Leicester—but at the last moment stood aside for another who had asked to serve in his place that night. The substitute was shot through the head. Bunyan lived to allure the hearts of men with his story of the Kingdom of God, *Pilgrim's Progress.*

So we might continue to cite apparently little incidents, to us chance events, upon which turned great events and issues. And so the lesson we learn from the pages of Esther is the lesson of Divine Providence.

In a particular sense, the story of Esther is a commentary on the history of the Jews. Haman after Haman has arisen to destroy them, but God always preserves them. Their oppressors fall and disappear. The eternal Jew goes on from age to age. God keeps His promise of old—"I will make a full end of the nations whither I have driven thee; but I will not make a full end of thee." Frederick once asked his chaplain to give him in a single sentence the proof of the existence of God. Back came the answer: "the Jew, Your Majesty."

Faith in the providence of God gives us confidence that the affairs of this troubled world are in His hands. He never lets go of the helm of His universe. His cause is always safe. His kingdom is an everlasting kingdom. Time's drama—world rising behind world, universe behind universe—is God's drama; and here on this planet the great men, great nations, races, empires, epochs, are but the brief embodiment and transient realization of His desires.

Faith in God's providence gives us strength and confidence in our own lives. If God is present by His providence in the lives of nations, then He must also be present in the lives of individuals— and that means you and me. God's engagements in the mighty affairs of the universe do not preclude His providential direction of our own personal destiny. The book of providence, like Hebrew, must be read backward. But when we look back we can see that God was there.

GOD HAS A PLAN FOR EVERY LIFE

The other great truth taught by the history of Esther is that God has a plan for every life. When Esther awoke to that fact, she was ready for any labor and any sacrifice. It was Mordecai who brought home to her that most impressive and important fact. Until then Esther was just another beautiful Hebrew girl, basking in the pleasures of Ahasuerus' harem.

She demurred when Mordecai asked her to go in and plead before the king for her people. She reminded him of the great risk to herself. It might cost her her life. She much preferred the warm light of the palace and the caresses of the king. But Mordecai reminded her that perhaps she had come to the throne for that very hour—"for such a time as this," for the crisis that was breaking, for the deliverance of her people from destruction.

When that idea sank into the mind of Esther, it transformed her from the soft, pleasure-loving beauty, unwilling to take any risk—even for the redemption of her race. She became one of the great heroines of all the ages, the woman who said, "I will go in unto the king; and if I perish, I perish."

What was true of Esther, beside the throne of the master of the world, is true of the humblest daughter of Eve, true of all of us. God has a purpose in our lives. For that particular purpose He has brought us to such a place, to such a time, to such an opportunity.

This is a mighty and an encouraging truth. It warns the careless and flippant, living butterfly lives, without any serious thought or desire or purpose, that life is a serious, earnest thing. Are you living today as if God had something that He brought you into the world to do? This truth also encourages those who are cast down, depressed, or disappointed in life, who are tempted to deplore the uselessness of their lives and their labors, and wonder if God has any place for them in His great plan. Be of good courage! God not only has a place for you in the working out of His great plan, but He has a particular plan in *your* life and a particular work for *you* to do. If you are obedient to Him, if you are trusting in Him, if you are serving Him, you are doing that work, even when you may think your life has no use or meaning.

Rise, then, to greatness of life! Choose God's side. When Esther understood, when she saw that God was calling her to a certain work, she rose magnificently to do it, leaving behind her, still ringing down the ages, her sublime resolution, "If I perish, I perish."

Paul said God has called all of us to glory and honor and immortality. Do you hear that? You are called to that great destiny—honor, glory, immortality. Are you living today as if that were true? God has sent His Son that we might have eternal life. Have you taken Christ? Have you made Him your Master? Are you following Him along the path that leads to that grand destiny, when, changed from glory into glory, we shall see Him as he is?

QUESTIONS FOR DISCUSSION:

1. As you see Esther and Vashti revealed in this chapter, which do you think has the most outstanding character?

2. Does Ahasuerus, the powerful king of Persia, have any modern counterparts? Discuss the character of this ancient monarch. Can you think of any modern rulers who have this kind of power?

3. Discuss the ramifications of this ancient "beauty pageant" won by Esther. Why do you think she stood out from the other "contestants"? Was Esther's guardian, Mordecai, right to enter her in the contest?

4. How could a man like Haman achieve the kind of power he had?

5. From its earliest days, the Israelite nation has been subject to much persecution. Why is this so, do you think?

6. Discuss the providence of God as revealed in the book of Esther. How could this be true in a book that does not even mention the name of God?

7. "God has a purpose in our lives." Discuss and apply the truth of this statement to your own life.

Editor's note: Read Joshua 2 as you prepare for this study. Also read an article on Rahab in a Bible Dictionary or Encyclopedia.

3

THE WOMAN WHO WAS BETTER THAN HER JOB

And she bound the scarlet line in the window　　(Josh. 2:21).

This woman's job was what has been called the oldest profession; and since it is also the lowest, the least said about it the better. In one of his hymns on faith, Frederick William Faber sings:

> O gift of gifts! O grace of faith!
> My God, how can it be
> That Thou, who hast discerning love,
> Shouldst give that gift to me?
> How many hearts Thou mightst have had
> More innocent than mine,
> How many souls more worthy far
> Of that sweet touch of Thine
> Ah, grace, into unlikeliest hearts
> It is thy boast to come;
> The glory of thy light to find
> In darkest spots a home.

When Rahab believed and was saved, that was the very song she might have sung, had it then been written, for, in truth, that was what happened in her case. She might well have wondered that God, who has discerning love, should have given that gift to her. She must have thought of the many hearts in Jericho which were far more worthy of that sweet touch of God's Holy Spirit.

To humble our pride and to teach us that we are saved by the grace of God, God took a harlot and by her teaches us the meaning of faith.

Climb with me now to this mountaintop on the other side the Jordan River. Israel's great leader, Moses, has finished his work. On Nebo's lonely mountain, in a vale in the land of Moab, Moses slept in his unknown grave. But before Moses died he laid his hands upon that valiant soldier, Joshua, and appointed him his successor. Moses has led the people out of Egypt, through the wanderings of the forty years in the burning deserts, and had brought them to the river Jordan, in the land of Moab. But to Joshua fell the dangerous and difficult task of taking the people over the river and conquering the land of Canaan.

Like a wise soldier and general, before he crosses the river and attacks Jericho Joshua makes a reconnaissance. There he stands on the top of the mountain looking off toward the land of Canaan. Far below him lies the encampment of Israel. In the center is the Tabernacle with the Ark of the Covenant. About the Tabernacle are encamped the twelve tribes of Israel—Levi, Judah, Simeon, Benjamin, Dan, Issachar, and the rest of them—their standards waving in the spring sunshine. Beyond the encampment flows the Jordan River, swollen with the spring rains and "overflowing all his banks."

Across the river lay the land of Canaan, forever now the Holy Land. There it lay; the land of Israel's future history, the stage of divine redemption; the land forever to be associated with Israel's patriarchs and kings and captains, prophets and apostles. Canaan is the vital site of Israel's conquests, apostasies, exiles, and restorations; her temple worship; and the fulfillment of the grand hopes and prophecies of God's people—the incarnation, the miracles, the crucifixion, the resurrection, the ascension into heaven, the outpouring of the Holy Spirit, and the beginning of the Christian church.

Beyond the river Joshua saw the fertile plain of the Jordan valley; to the north the Sea of Galilee, and to the south the Dead Sea. Yonder is Jericho with her thick walls and towering ramparts; and yonder the mountain eminence, the Jebusite stronghold, which will be known and forever venerated by mankind as Jerusalem. To the south of that mount lies Bethlehem, where Christ will be born; and far in the distance Joshua can see the gleam and flash of the Great Sea itself. This was the "goodly land" he was to conquer.

JOURNEY TO JERICHO

Calling to him two soldiers of proven courage and character, Joshua points out to them the stronghold of Jericho, directly across the river, and tells them he wants them to explore the city. They are to bring him a report of its walls and gates, its state of preparation, the number of its inhabitants, the size of its army. "Go view the land, even Jericho." It was a difficult and dangerous assignment. But that evening, when night had come down, the two men set forth.

An interesting tradition has it that Salmon, who afterward married Rahab, was one of the spies. If so, this finishing touch of romance makes the story of Rahab one of the most fascinating in the Bible. First they crossed the flooded Jordan and then made their way, probably in the disguise of merchants, to Jericho, where they passed through the gates of the city, and, asking for the house of a harlot—for merchants frequently made such houses their stopping places—they were directed to the home of Rahab.

In spite of their disguise, the presence of the two strangers in Jericho at once aroused suspicion, especially in view of the common knowledge of the near approach of the host of Israel. Officers of the king watched where the two men went and at once reported their whereabouts to their master. The king immediately dispatched soldiers to take them. When the soldiers came to Rahab's door, they said to her, "Bring forth the men that are come to thee, which are entered into thine house; for they be come to search out all the country" (Josh. 2:3).

REACHING RAHAB'S HEART

But instead of producing the strangers, Rahab hid them and
protected them. She immediately discerned that these two men
were different from others who had come to her home. They
were perhaps the first who had not entered it for sinful purposes.
The Spirit of God, unaided, could have produced in the harlot's
heart the impression that these men represented God and His
cause, and therefore must not be molested; but it is more likely
that, as He often does, the Holy Spirit worked that night through
human agents. These men spoke to Rahab of the God of Israel,
and of the great destiny of the people of God. What they told her
reached her heart, and she believed the spies. Rahab must have felt
that her great hour had struck, and that it was her God-appointed
destiny to hide the spies and to help the people of Israel and serve
the God of Israel.

Since these men represented God's holy cause, she determined
to protect and save them from the wrath of the king of Jericho. So
a harlot became God's servant and messenger when the soldiers
came pounding on her door. She told them that two men—from
where, she knew not—had come to her house that day; but about
the time for the shutting of the gates of the city they had gone
their way—whither, she knew not. "But," she said to the soldiers,
"it is such a short time since they departed that you will have no
trouble in coming up with them if you pursue hastily" (see Josh.
2:5). Supposing that the two men had taken the road back to the
fords of the Jordan, the soldiers hurried off in that direction.

It was a vain chase; for all the time the spies of Joshua were
hiding on the roof of Rahab's house, where, upon the first appearance of the soldiers to inquire after them, she had hid them under
the stalks of flax which were drying there. Like Lydia, the purple
seller of Thyatira, who became the first convert to Christianity in
Europe when Paul preached at Philippi, Rahab, the first convert
to Judaism from the heathen world, seems to have been a dyer and
a seller of linen, as well as a harlot.

As soon as the soldiers were out of hearing, Rahab went up to
the housetop. A great wave of penitence, of yearning for a higher
life, and a thirst after God, undoubtedly filled the heart of Rahab
that night. There, on the roof of the house, in the silence of the

night, with the stars looking down upon the heathen city which lay all quiet about her, and the grim mountains rising in the distance, their harshness softened in the evening shadows, Rahab made to the spies her great confession of faith. She told them she knew that God had given the city and the land to Israel, for she had heard of their mighty conquests on the way up from Egypt. There were other gods, the cruel and licentious gods of Jericho and Canaan; but she was convinced, she said, that the only true God was the God of Israel. "For the Lord your God, he is God in heaven above, and in earth beneath" (Josh. 2:11).

The spies had come to investigate the strength of Jericho and its mighty walls, reports concerning which had reached Joshua and his army. But that night they listened to earnest words from the erstwhile heathen lips of a woman who tells them how strong God is in Israel. So the heathen harlot strengthens the faith of the Hebrew spies in their own God!

Later on, when Gideon still feared to attack the host of Midian with his army of 300 men, God told him to go down that night into the host of Midian, and "thou shalt hear what they say" (Judges 7:11). That night, listening against one of the black tents of the Midianites, Gideon heard one of them relate his dream to his fellow—the dream of the barley loaf that came tumbling down and knocked over the tent. The interpretation given that dream was that God would deliver Midian into the hands of Gideon. Thus strengthened, Gideon went back and led his army to its great victory. Yes, "thou shalt hear what they say!"

Often in the camp of unbelief, in the world which appears so hostile to the church, there are spoken secret appraisals of the strength and the influence of the church, of Christ, His Cross and the godly life, which, if we could listen to them, would hearten us and strengthen our faith.

RAHAB'S CONFESSION OF FAITH

"For the Lord your God, he is God in heaven above, and in earth beneath," said Rahab (Josh. 2:11). Considering the time, the place, the hour, the circumstances, and that it was a harlot who made it, this is one of the most remarkable confessions of faith in the Bible. And it is not strange that, ages after, the faith that inspired it is spoken of along with that of Abraham and Moses and Enoch and Noah.

Her first request is not for herself, but for her father's house. Like all noble souls she was concerned for the welfare of others. Rahab did not care to be saved alone. In return for her kindness to the spies she begs that they will show kindness to her father's house, and asks that they seal their promise with a sign and token. The spies assured her that if she followed their directions her life and the lives of all her father's household would be saved.

Then Rahab took one of the scarlet ropes which she had dyed and which she used in her business, and binding it about the waist of one of the spies, she lowered him from the window to the ground below. The rope was released by the first spy and drawn up again to the window by Rahab, who quickly bound it about the waist of the second spy, and in the same manner lowered him safely to the ground. This was in order that they would not have to pass out of the gate of the city and thus risk capture and death.

Then the two men called up to Rahab to bind the rope to the window, letting it hang down over the wall, and when the city was attacked by Joshua's army, his soldiers, informed in advance, would spare her house and all her people when they saw that scarlet rope hanging from the window.

Then the two men departed, and at the wise advice of Rahab, instead of starting back at once toward the Jordan, went into the mountains west of Jericho. There they lay hidden for three days, and then retraced their steps across the Jordan to make their report to Joshua. When Joshua heard the remarkable story of Rahab, he felt sure that God would give him the victory in the coming battle, "Truly the Lord hath delivered into our hands all the land" (Josh. 2:24).

As soon as the sun was up the next morning, Rahab hurried through the streets to the home of her father and mother. It may have been that she had never crossed the threshold of that home since she took up her sinful calling, and we can imagine the joy and surprise of the father and mother when they saw their long-lost daughter return. But it was not a time for rejoicing. Rahab said to them: "Come with me! The army of the Israelites, led by Jehovah, will surely take and destroy Jericho and all its people; but I have secured a promise from the Hebrew spies, whom I hid from the king's soldiers, that if I hang the scarlet thread from the window of my house they will spare me and all my family. Come with me!" And all her kindred who believed her word followed her back through the streets and took refuge in her house, high up on the wall of the city.

When, after the miraculous crossing of the Jordan, the army of Israel moved against Jericho, Joshua gave strict orders that in the general destruction of the city and its inhabitants Rahab and all her household were to be spared, because she had hid the spies and confessed her faith in the God of Israel. For six days the people, in ominous silence, save for the blast of the priests on the rams' horns, marched around the prodigious walls of Jericho, while the defenders looked down and jeered from the ramparts of the city.

As Joshua's army encircled the city on those successive days, I can see Rahab standing at the window, watching the army as it marches past, and back of her are her father and mother, her brothers and sisters, and all her kindred. The spies, too, were in that army, and perhaps they waved a greeting to Rahab when they saw her standing at the window where the scarlet cord was floating in the breeze.

On the seventh day they encircled the city seven times; and when, on the seventh round, the priests sounded with their horns, the walls of Jericho fell flat and the army of Joshua rushed into the doomed city with drawn swords. The fearful work of vengeance and destruction was complete. But through the carnage and the debris and the dust of fallen structures, the two spies made their way quickly in the direction of the house of Rahab. In the window they saw the red cord which Rahab, faithful to their directions, had hung there. Entering into the house and going up to the chamber on the wall, the spies tied the rope about Rahab and lowered her to a place of safety amid the army of Israel. Then her father and mother and all her kindred were lowered to safety in the same way.

The same scarlet rope that had saved the spies saved Rahab. Ever afterward she dwelt with the people of Israel; and in the table of our Lord's ancestors in Matthew's Gospel (cf. Matt. 1:5) Rahab, the wife of Salmon, is the mother of Boaz. Thus, Rahab the harlot had the high honor of being one of our Lord's ancestors. That, in brief, is the story of Rahab the harlot, the woman who was better than her job.

BEAUTY IN STRANGE PLACES

The history of Rahab is, in the first place, a striking illustration of the fact that beauty of character and Christian faith may be planted of God in most unlikely places. There must have been hundreds of virtuous women in Jericho then, but all were passed over by the electing grace of God for a harlot. Rahab was capable of a faith that receives mention from age to age.

That was something that our Lord Himself liked to emphasize and show—the beautiful possibilities of a soul even in the lowest state. So He said that publicans and harlots would go into the kingdom of heaven before many self-righteous persons who thought they had no need of salvation.

Rahab's story is a tribute to the possibilities of every human soul. The woman who was a sinner lives forever in Christian memory, for Christ found a place in her darkest heart. The masters of human thought and fiction have liked to dwell upon this high capacity of the most unlikely lives. Among instances we think of are Quasimodo in Victor Hugo's *Notre Dame*, and Miriam in Charles Kingsley's *Hypatia*. Kingsley thus eloquently describes the better woman in the heart of that witch and panderer:

Her grim, withered features grew softer, purer, grander, and rose ennobled for a moment to their long-lost might-have-been, to that personal ideal which every soul brings with it into the world, which shines dim and potential in the face of every sleeping babe, before it has been scarred and distorted and encrusted in the long tragedy of life. Sorceress she was, panderer and slave dealer, steeped to the lips in falsehood, ferocity, and avarice, yet that paltry stone brought home to her some thought, true, spiritual, impalpable, unmarketable, before which all her treasures and all her ambitions were as worthless in her own eyes as they were in the eyes of the angels of God.

THE POWER OF DECISION FOR GOD

Again in the history of Rahab we see the importance and the power of decision for God. In the divine goodness of God, the knowledge of the true God and the way of life was presented to her by those spies who had come to her house. Rahab was not only convinced, but *acted* upon her convictions and chose the destiny of the people of God. She was not only impressed, but *acted* at once upon her impressions; disregarding the personal risk involved, she hid and protected the two spies, and then made her confession of faith and her irrevocable decision.

Where a firm decision for God is made in a human life, there the foundation of all future success and strength is laid; but where there is no firm decision, no matter what earnest and deep impressions and desires there may be, the fruits of the Christian life will never make their appearance.

Balaam, like Rahab, knew that God was with the Israelites. He was impressed with their future destiny and desired to share in that destiny. When he was hired by the kings of Moab to curse the invaders, instead of cursing them he blessed them in terms of incomparable eloquence, and made his celebrated prayer, "Let me die the death of the righteous, and let my last end be like his" (see Numbers 23:10).

But his longing was not followed by decision and choice. Unlike Rahab, he was not willing to pay the price, and, lured by the gold of Moab, instead of dying the death of a servant of God, he died miserably in battle against the people of God (see Numbers 31:8).

Your feelings may be all right; but without decision and choice those feelings will be as vain as the summer wind. You believe in God, in Christ, in His atonement on the cross, in the heavenly life to come. But does your life show that by your daily confession? Have you separated yourself from the world, as Rahab separated herself from the people of Jericho and chose the people of God?

SAVING FAITH

What the Bible emphasizes about Rahab however—and it always emphasizes the great thing—is her faith. In that grand roll call of the heroes and heroines of faith in Hebrews 11, the name of Rahab the harlot is forever inscribed. "By faith the harlot Rahab perished not with them that believed not, when she had received the spies with peace" (Heb. 11:31).

What were the characteristics of the faith of Rahab that make it worthy of such high mention? It was faith where all others did not believe. All the other inhabitants of Jericho must have jeered and scoffed at Joshua's army, when it marched around the walls of the heathen stronghold. Only Rahab looked upon that army in faith and believed that God was with it. It was faith that counted all else to be loss save that in which she put her faith. It was faith that showed itself by works, without which our faith is dead.

She believed in God and in the destiny of the people of God; and she matched her faith by her works, for she hid and protected the spies. James does not contradict the statement of the Hebrews or the statement of Paul that Rahab was saved by faith, when he asks, "Likewise also was not Rahab the harlot justified by works, when she had received the messengers, and had sent them out another way?" (James 2:25). You believe in God; you trust in Christ; you accept the glorious destiny of the redeemed. But do you back up that faith by your works, by your daily life?

THE SCARLET CORD AND THE BLOOD OF CHRIST

It is not strange that in the scarlet cord waving from the window of Rahab's house of Jericho's wall when the city was being destroyed by the army of Joshua, and which saved her and her household, Christian faith should have seen a symbol of the saving power of the Cross of Christ, and faith in that Cross. How could a waving scarlet cord save Rahab's house from the doom of Jericho?

There was certainly nothing in the situation of Rahab's house which guaranteed its safety, for it stood high up on the wall, in the most dangerous place of all. How could a scarlet thread save that house? Yet it did. How can our faith in the Cross of Christ, that scarlet cord of mercy which God has flung out from the windows of heaven, save us from death and reconcile us to God and bless our lives with unending joy and happiness hereafter? Yet that is the promise of the Word of God.

Have you taken God at His word when He says, "He that

believeth . . . . shall be saved"? Is the scarlet thread of the Cross, of Christ's blood, over your soul? Is it over your home and your household? Are you concerned for your household as Rahab was for hers?

I can show you the spot in our old home where our mother offered her daily prayers for her children. Can you mothers show me the spot in your home where you pray for your children? Will they be able to go back to the old home—your children—and say, "There mother prayed for me"? Is the scarlet thread of your faith in the redeeming blood of Christ waving in the window of your soul?

God has made His eternal promise that he that believeth in the Lord Jesus Christ shall be saved. He will keep that promise as faithfully as Joshua did when he destroyed Jericho, but spared the house of Rahab the harlot, where the scarlet cord was waving. Is the cord there today? Are you trusting in the Cross? One day the trumpets of judgment will sound, as they sounded of old over ancient and doomed Jericho. But where the scarlet cord waves, there is safety and refuge. "The blood of Jesus Christ His Son cleanseth us from all sin."

QUESTIONS FOR DISCUSSION:

1. Discuss the character of Rahab as revealed in Joshua 2 and any other sources you might have. Can you think of any modern day "Rahabs" in your acquaintance?

2. Read Hebrews 11:31 and discuss its implications for a study of this Bible woman.

3. While the names of the two Hebrew spies are not given, what kind of men do you think they were in view of Rahab's reaction to them and recognition of their God? What else do you think influenced her thinking?

4. Was Rahab justified in lying about the whereabouts of the spies (see verse 5)? Can you think of more recent events that have called for this kind of behavior among believers?

5. Has your faith ever been encouraged by a "younger" believer?

6. What does Rahab's concern for her family tell you about her?

7. Why is Rahab's faith so remarkable?

Editor's Note: Compare Lot's wife to Ruth, who was a later descendant of Lot through his first-born daughter who gave birth to Moab after her mother's death.

4

THE WOMAN TO REMEMBER

But his wife looked back from behind him,
and she became a pillar of salt   (Genesis 19:26)

In His teaching and preaching, our Lord handed down to immortality of fame two women. One was that woman who anointed His head and feet with costly ointment and dried His feet with the hair of her head. Of that woman Jesus said that wherever His Gospel should be preached throughout the whole world what she had done would be spoken of as a memorial of her. And that has come to pass. Again today, in a part of the world not then known to be in existence, the name of that woman is mentioned.

The other was Lot's wife, who turned back and became a pillar of salt. In the midst of one of His sermons, when He was speaking of the separations and sacrifices which true religion requires of the soul, Jesus suddenly uttered that solemn warning. "Remember Lot's wife." It is Christ Himself, then, who singles out, among all the women of the Old Testament, Lot's wife as one whose fate is to be studied and remembered by every Christian who is in earnest about the salvation of his soul.

This is all that is told us of Lot's wife: she looked back and became a pillar of salt, and Christ made use of her doom to illustrate His sermon. But that is enough. All the rest it is not

45

difficult to fill in. Lot's wife looked back because the world she had come to love was in Sodom. There was her treasure, and there her heart also.

Let us review a little of the history of Lot and his family before this event, when his wife perished as Sodom was burning. Lot was the nephew of Abraham. His herdsmen had fought with the herdsmen of Abraham over places of pasturage. Instead of backing up his herdsmen and continuing the quarrel, Abraham suggested that he and Lot and their followers and flocks should separate, each choosing a section of the country as his dwelling place.

With characteristic generosity, Abraham gave Lot the first choice. Lot saw that the most fertile part of the country was the valley of the Jordan. He must have known that it bordered the wicked cities of Sodom and Gomorrah, but he no doubt felt he could take care of himself and keep his family uncontaminated by the wickedness of those cities. Therefore, he chose the land toward the south and pitched his tent toward Sodom.

Take note of that! He pitched his tent *toward* Sodom. He did not take up his abode *in* Sodom, neither did he settle down close to its walls; but he pitched his tent *toward* Sodom. That was the section where he chose his territory, and it was the general direction in which his encampment looked.

There are many who are not yet in the Sodom of wickedness and denial of God. Their names are not yet inscribed on the roll of the citizens of that place. But there is a certain set of the sails of their life, a certain tone and color and inclination—a pitch of their tent, which is in the direction of Sodom.

What about you? Are you pitching your tent toward Sodom? Are you going along with the world rather than with the church? Are you inclining more to the people of Sodom than to the people of God? Then take heed lest you become a full-fledged citizen of Sodom. That was what happened to Lot and his wife.

The cup of Sodom's iniquity was not full to overflowing. "Wheresoever the carcass is," said Christ, "there will the eagles be gathered together" (Matt. 24:28). There is a "thus far and no farther" with God, and when men or nations cross that line, then come the vultures of judgment and retribution. When the angels told Abraham of the approaching doom of Sodom and Gomorrah, he pleaded with God to spare the cities. He received from God the promise that if Sodom could muster ten righteous men He would not destroy the city. But because that many, or few, righteous men could not be found in the place, God looses the thunderbolts of His wrath and judgment.

LOST INFLUENCE

The one righteous man, however, that there was in Sodom, and his family, received a warning in time to be saved. When Lot learned the coming doom of the city, he at once went to speak to his sons-in-law, and said to them, "Up, get you out of this place; for the Lord will destroy this city" (Gen. 19:14).

But Lot had lived too long in Sodom to be taken seriously. His sons-in-law thought he was joking. "He seemed to them as one that mocked" (Gen. 19:14). And just before that, when Lot had rebuked the men of Sodom for the terrible and shameful proposal they made concerning the angels who had come to warn him—a fearful sin which has taken its name from Sodom—they said one to another, "This one fellow came in to sojourn, and he will needs be a judge!" (Gen. 19:9). What they meant was, "Who is this Lot, who dwells in Sodom, has chosen it for his abode, and now preaches morality to us!" (Gen. 19:9).

Thus Lot had lost his influence, both with his sons-in-law and with the citizens of Sodom. When he wishes to be taken seriously, they think he is mocking. He seemed to them as one who mocked! What is sadder than the passing of influence? And how easily it passes. The wrong kind of a glance, the wrong kind of a word, the little mean advantage, the lack of earnestness or sincerity, a little departure from the truth, and our power to influence some immortal soul for eternal life is ruined and lost. We seem to them as one who mocks.

WHEN DEATH STRIKES

All Lot could persuade to leave the city with him were his wife and his two daughters. Imagination staggers when we try to picture the doom that fell upon those towns. At Pompeii the visitor looks upon the lava-encased bodies of those who perished in the great eruption of Vesuvius, and gets some idea of the terrors of that disaster and judgment. There they lie, just as they were, and at the very work in which they were engaged when the fiery flood overflowed them.

So it must have been at Sodom and Gomorrah. The peasant was plowing with the oxen in the fields near the city; the baker was at work before his oven; the priest was ministering in the temple before his idols; the merchant was counting his money and taking an inventory of his goods; the housewife was busy in her kitchen; the scribe was writing with his pen; the rich man was driving by in his chariot; the beggar had his hand out for an alms; the thief, the drunkard, and the adulterer were in the midst of their sins, when death overtook them.

An appalling disaster and judgment. And yet, was there anything singular about that? Is not that the way death always comes? It stops men in their tracks. It stops the preacher in his pulpit, the scholar in his study, the soldier in his battle, the lover in his embrace, the singer in his music, the farmer in his furrow, the good man in his good work, and the wicked man in his deed of wickedness.

Just as we are, death takes us. Then there can be no change, no alteration, and what we have written we have written. Let us live, then, in the light of truth, and be ready for the touch of that hand which, so far as this world and its opportunities, its hopes, its sorrows, its disappointments, its ambitions, its transgressions, and its fears are concerned, arrests and stops us forever.

A FATAL LOOK

The angels who took Lot and his wife by the hand and led them out of the city said to him, "Escape for thy life; look not behind thee, neither stay thou in all the plain; escape to the mountain, lest thou be consumed" (Gen. 19:17). But as they journeyed toward the mountain, Lot's wife, disregarding the injunction of the angels, stopped and, turning, looked toward the doomed cities. That moment she became a pillar of salt.

The fate of Lot's wife has an interesting counterpart, although altogether different in the lesson which it teaches, in the ancient myth of Orpheus. Orpheus was the most famous musician of his day, and when he played upon his lyre not only his fellow mortals but even wild animals were softened and subdued by his melodious strains. The very trees and rocks were sensible to the charm of his music.

When his wife Eurydice, fleeing from the shepherd Aristaeus, was bitten in the foot by a snake and died, Orpheus resolved to seek his wife in the regions of the dead. With his lyre he went through the realms of Pluto, and sang in such tender and mournful strains that even the very ghosts shed tears. Tantalus ceased for a moment in his efforts for water. Ixion's wheel stood still. The daughters of Danaus rested from their task of drawing water in a sieve, and Sisyphus sat on his rock to listen.

Pluto at length gave his consent for Eurydice to return with Orpheus to the upper air, but upon condition that he should not turn round and look upon her until they had emerged from Hades. Through all the horrors of hell they passed safely, and were on the very verge of the light of the upper air when Orpheus, "unmindful of fate, alas! and soul subdued, looked back." That moment Eurydice became a ghost again. So a soul's happiness may be lost by one backward glance.

Lot's wife was *almost* saved; yet she was lost because she looked back. We speak of her as a "socialite who became salt," because in many ways she is a type of those women, and men too, who start out on the Christian life, accept in general the great truths of Christianity, but, because their hearts have never been changed, go back and perish.

THE HEART AND ITS TREASURE

Lot's wife's heart was in Sodom because her treasure was there. When Lot moved into Sodom, I have no doubt it was at the urging of his wife. The life in the city appealed to her far more than the roving existence in the black tents, with the smell of sheep and goats and camels always about her. In the city she became a fine lady, lived in a mansion on Main Street, met with the other select women in their homes, was pointed out as Lot's wife. It was not strange that she wanted to remain in Sodom with all its pleasures.

When Lot first made the announcement that they must get out of the city, his wife, I suppose, begged him to stay. She pointed to the sky, asking Lot to show where there was even the smallest cloud to indicate the coming storm. Why be upset by the word of two men he had never seen before? Probably it was a scheme to get him out of the city so that others might seize his property.

"This fine house, Lot—do you want me to leave it for one of those black tents and become a wandering Bedouin again? Why should I give up my comforts here, all my costly, fashionable gowns, and the friends I have made here? And there are our daughters. Their husbands will not go with them. They know only the city life, and they are just getting into the higher social circles of Sodom."

HALFWAY CHRISTIANS

Yet, despite her protests, Lot persuaded her to accompany him from the city. In that respect she is like many others who come into the church and start the Christian life, but half unwillingly, and with no joy or conviction or desire. Some distance from the city, Lot's wife again, I suppose, besieged him with her complaints and voiced her desire to go back. But Lot reminded her of what the angels had said and urged her to go on. On, then, with heavy, dragging feet, she went.

As a rule, it is the husband who is a dead weight on the spiritual life of the wife, but here it is the wife who tries to hold her husband back. Among the saddest experiences of the minister are those homes where a wife holds back a husband in his religious life, keeps him from church, and, unless he has sufficient independence and courage, will keep him out of the Kingdom of Heaven.

That, I say, is one of the saddest spectacles that the minister ever beholds. And whenever he sees it he thinks of Lot's wife. So far as turning back and looking back were concerned, Lot's wife might just as well do so, for her heart had already looked back—and out of the heart are the issues of life.

THE NEW BIRTH

Thus we come back to that fundamental necessity of every true Christian life—the new birth. It is as essential to spiritual life as physical birth is to physical life. "Except a man be born again," said the Author of all spiritual life, "he cannot see the kingdom of God" (John 3:3). But when we say a man *must* be born again, we never say it without also saying a man *can* or a woman *can* be born again. That is the glorious possibility for us all.

ONLY ONE LOOK!

It was just one look that Lot's wife took, and yet by that one look she became a pillar of salt. In a moment of time, in the yielding or acquiescence of a single second, irreparable injury can be done to the soul. Only one look from his palace roof at a woman bathing on the roof of another house, and King David—God-loving, psalm-singing David, he who strikes every chord in the heart of man—went staggering and reeling and plunging down into the abyss of his sin.

Who can measure the possibilities for good or evil in a moment of time? In a moment of time the devil showed Christ the kingdoms of this world and their glory, and asked for his worship; and in that same moment of time Christ won the victory and said, "Get thee behind me, Satan."

If by only one look, if in only one moment of time, a deep injury can be wrought to the soul, it is equally true that in the resistance of a moment of time, in the choice of a moment of time, in the earnest heartfelt prayer of a moment of time, temptation can be conquered and eternal life secured. How eloquent, and also how moving and pathetic, was that last prayer of blind Samson, as they led him forth to make sport for the Philistines in the temple of Dagon. "O Lord God, remember me, I pray thee, and strengthen me, I pray thee, *only this once*" (Judges 16:28). By an "only this once"—one foolish yielding to the blandishments of the lovely siren Delilah—Samson had been cast into slavery and blindness. Now he asked God to remember him, "only this once." That prayer was granted, and by one final great exploit for God the past transgressions of Samson were atoned.

WHEN ANGELS TAKE US BY THE HAND

Lot's wife had many advantages, yet she was lost. She had a godly husband, still uncontaminated by the society of Sodom, yet she was lost. She had the memories of her association with godly Abraham, yet she was lost. She had the warning of the angels and the pleading of her husband, yet she was lost. She had, too, the special intervention of the angels. They took her hand and her husband by the hand. Yes, angels took her by the hand. Yet Lot's wife was lost.

Lot's wife was not the only woman, not the only person, whom angels have taken by the hand. I invoke now to your memory and your conscience some of those angels who have taken you by the hand: the memory of a godly father, of a praying mother, who never once looked back on her heavenward journey; the sense, the feeling of the emptiness, the nothingness of much that this world holds and pursues; the sorrow that came over you when a loved one of your circle was laid in the grave; the pangs that conscience inflicted upon you when you sinned; the sigh and longing for a better life that once escaped your heart and your lips; the weariness or weakness of the flesh which revealed to you that your strength was not forever, and that before long you too must go the way of all the earth; the moving of the heart as you listened to sermon, song, or prayer that spoke of Christ's undying love for sinners.

What are these but God's angels taking you by the hand to lead you from the city of danger and death to the City of Life? Yes! angels of Jesus are they; angels of light, seeking to bring the pilgrim safe home to heaven. May those angels not take us by the hand in vain! Come, holy, compassionate angels! Take us by the hand and lead us out of the plains of sin and danger to the high tablelands of peace and safety. Lead us from our follies, our waywardness, our transgressions, into the presence of God, our Father!

QUESTIONS FOR DISCUSSION:

1. React to Dr. Macartney's premise: "Lot's wife looked back because the world she had come to love was in Sodom." What are the implications of this statement? When is it good to "look back"?

2. What do you think is Lot's responsibility in this whole matter?

3. Why had he lost his influence on his wife and family?

4. Discuss Dr. Macartney's statement: "Lot's wife was *almost* saved; yet she was lost because she looked back." Can you think of other Bible characters who were lost because they looked back?

5. What are some of the decisions people make in a moment of time which haunt (or help) them for the rest of their lives?

6. What one primary lesson have you learned from Lot's wife? Why should her story appear in a series on "great women of the Bible"?